Write Smart

ISBN: 978-1-897457-69-6

Contents

WriteSmart

Alphabet

Aa	4 – 5
Bb	6 – 7
Cc	8 – 9
Dd	10 – 11
Ee	12 – 13
Ff	14 – 15
Gg	16 – 17
Hh	18 – 19
Ii	20 – 21
Jj	22 – 23
Kk	24 – 25
Ll	26 – 27
Mm	28 – 29
Take a Break	30 – 31

ISBN: 978-1-897457-69-6

Nn   32 – 33
Oo   34 – 35
Pp   36 – 37
Qq   38 – 39
Rr   40 – 41
Ss   42 – 43
Tt   44 – 45
Uu   46 – 47
Vv   48 – 49
Ww   50 – 51
Xx   52 – 53
Yy   54 – 55
Zz   56 – 57
Take a Break   58 – 59

Vegetables   60 – 64

ISBN: 978-1-897457-69-6

Aa Bb Cc Dd Ee Ff Gg Hh Ii Jj Kk Ll Mm

alligator

Trace and write the letters.

ISBN: 978-1-897457-69-6

a

alien

a

bear

Trace and write the letters.

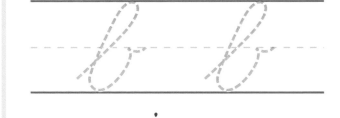

ISBN: 978-1-897457-69-6

beaver

Aa Bb Cc Dd Ee Ff Gg Hh Ii Jj Kk Ll Mm

cat

Trace and write the letters.

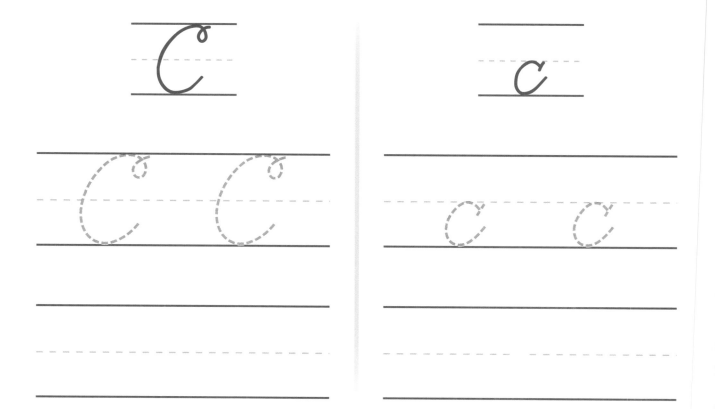

ISBN: 978-1-897457-69-6

cactus

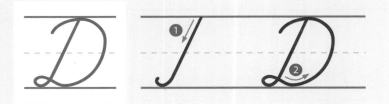

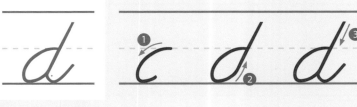

dinosaur

Trace and write the letters.

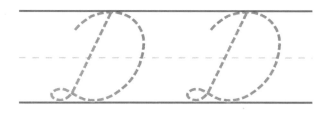

ISBN: 978-1-897457-69-6

D

d

dolphin

Aa Bb Cc Dd Ee Ff Gg Hh Ii Jj Kk Ll Mm

elf

Trace and write the letters.

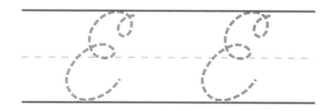

ISBN: 978-1-897457-69-6

elephant

Aa Bb Cc Dd Ee **Ff** Gg Hh Ii Jj Kk Ll Mm

fairy

Trace and write the letters.

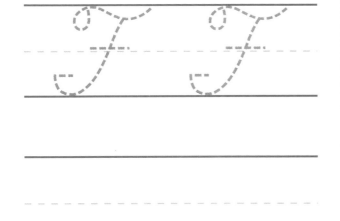

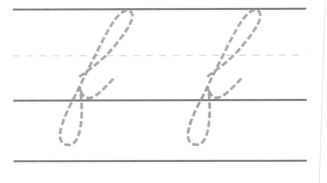

ISBN: 978-1-897457-69-6

flamingo

Aa Bb Cc Dd Ee Ff *Gg* Hh Ii Jj Kk Ll Mm

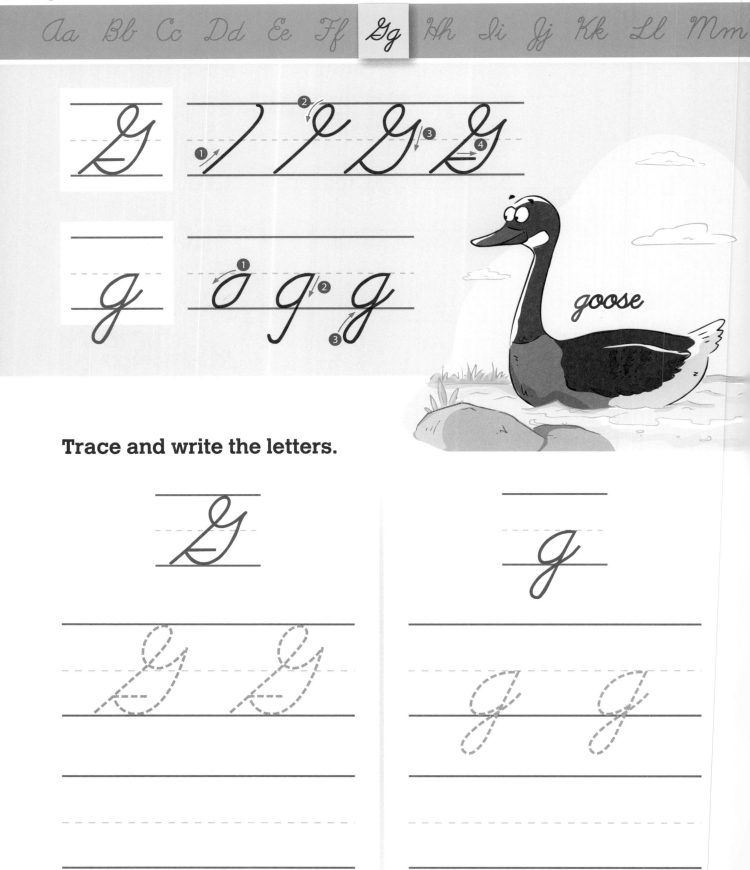

goose

Trace and write the letters.

ISBN: 978-1-897457-69-6

giraffe

ISBN: 978-1-897457-69-6

Aa Bb Cc Dd Ee Ff Gg Hh Ii Jj Kk Ll Mm

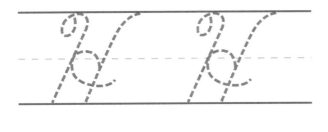

Trace and write the letters.

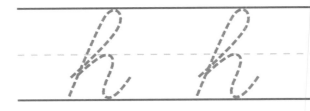

ISBN: 978-1-897457-69-6

hedgehog

ISBN: 978-1-897457-69-6

Aa Bb Cc Dd Ee Ff Gg Hh Ii Jj Kk Ll Mm

iron

Trace and write the letters.

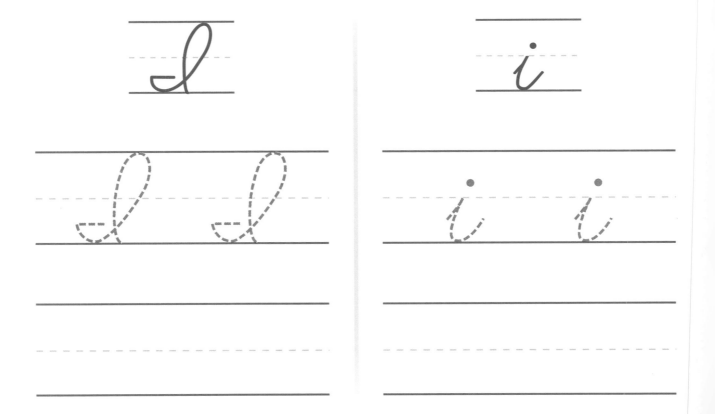

ISBN: 978-1-897457-69-6

ice cream

ISBN: 978-1-897457-69-6

Aa Bb Cc Dd Ee Ff Gg Hh Ii Jj Kk Ll Mm

jack-in-the-box

Trace and write the letters.

ISBN: 978-1-897457-69-6

jack-o'-lantern

ISBN: 978-1-897457-69-6

Aa Bb Cc Dd Ee Ff Gg Hh Ii Jj **Kk** Ll Mm

koala

Trace and write the letters.

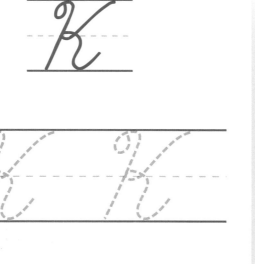

ISBN: 978-1-897457-69-6

kangaroos

Aa Bb Cc Dd Ee Ff Gg Hh Ii Jj Kk **Ll** *Mm*

ladybug

Trace and write the letters.

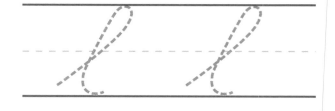

ISBN: 978-1-897457-69-6

lobster

Aa Bb Cc Dd Ee Ff Gg Hh Ii Jj Kk Ll **Mm**

mushroom

Trace and write the letters.

ISBN: 978-1-897457-69-6

monkey

ISBN: 978-1-897457-69-6

Aa Bb Cc Dd Ee Ff Gg Hh Ii Jj Kk Ll Mm

narwhals

Trace and write the letters.

ISBN: 978-1-897457-69-6

necklace

Aa Bb Cc Dd Ee Ff Gg Hh Ii Jj Kk Ll Mm

ostrich

Trace and write the letters.

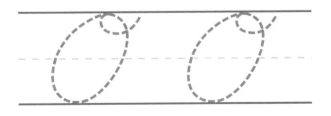

ISBN: 978-1-897457-69-6

octopus

ISBN: 978-1-897457-69-6

Aa Bb Cc Dd Ee Ff Gg Hh Ii Jj Kk Ll Mm

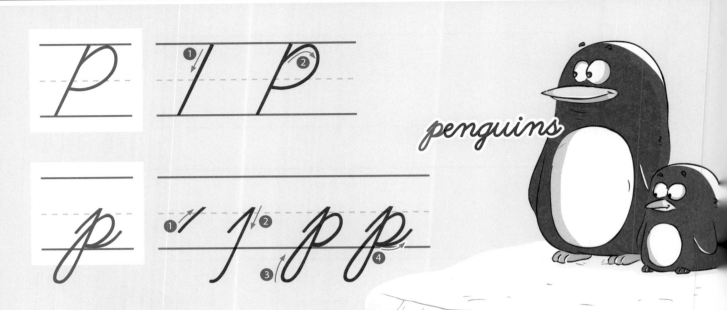

penguins

Trace and write the letters.

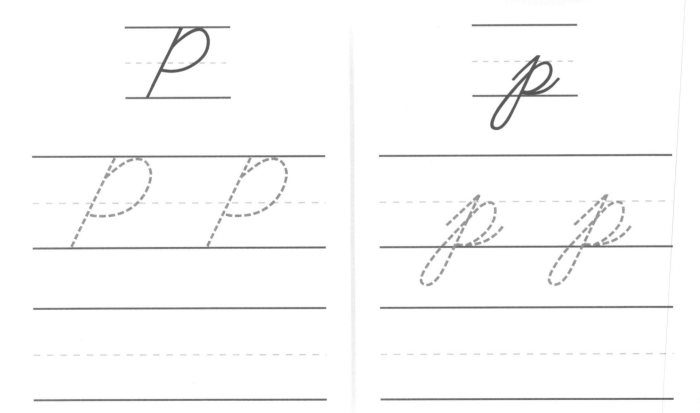

ISBN: 978-1-897457-69-6

parrot

Aa Bb Cc Dd Ee Ff Gg Hh Ii Jj Kk Ll Mm

quill

Trace and write the letters.

ISBN: 978-1-897457-69-6

Nn Oo Pp **Qq** Rr Ss Tt Uu Vv Ww Xx Yy Zz

quilt

ISBN: 978-1-897457-69-6   WriteSmart **39**

Aa Bb Cc Dd Ee Ff Gg Hh Ii Jj Kk Ll Mm

raccoon

Trace and write the letters.

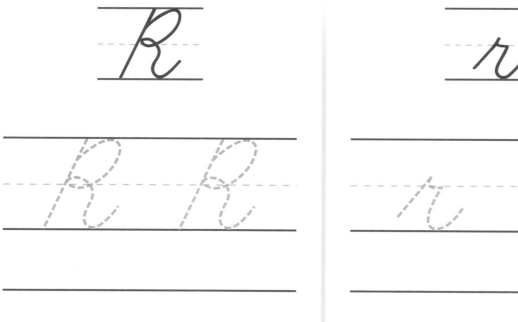

ISBN: 978-1-897457-69-6

rocket

Aa Bb Cc Dd Ee Ff Gg Hh Ii Jj Kk Ll Mm

Santa Claus

Trace and write the letters.

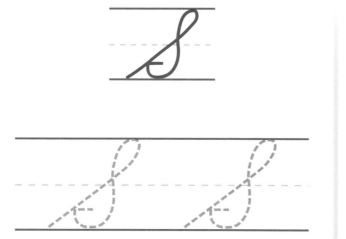

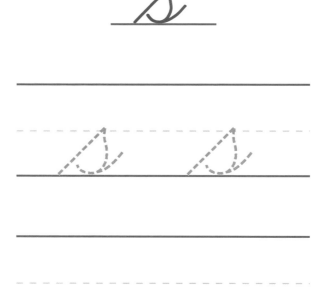

ISBN: 978-1-897457-69-6

snowman

Aa Bb Cc Dd Ee Ff Gg Hh Ii Jj Kk Ll Mm

tiger

Trace and write the letters.

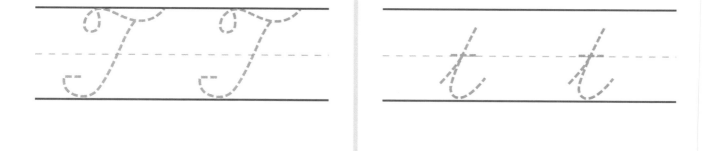

ISBN: 978-1-897457-69-6

tulip

Aa Bb Cc Dd Ee Ff Gg Hh Ii Jj Kk Ll Mm

unicorn

Trace and write the letters.

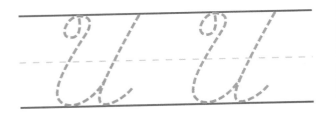

ISBN: 978-1-897457-69-6

umbrella

Trace and write the letters.

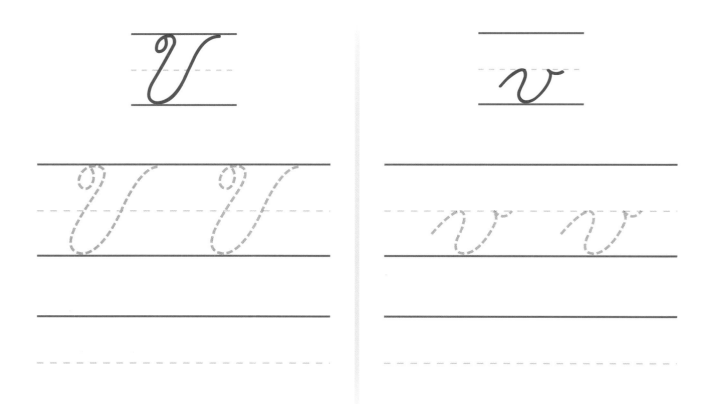

ISBN: 978-1-897457-69-6

volleyball

witch

Trace and write the letters.

ISBN: 978-1-897457-69-6

windmill

x-ray

Trace and write the letters.

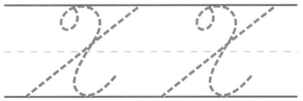

ISBN: 978-1-897457-69-6

xylophone

Aa Bb Cc Dd Ee Ff Gg Hh Ii Jj Kk Ll Mm

yacht

Trace and write the letters.

ISBN: 978-1-897457-69-6

yogurt

zucchini

Trace and write the letters.

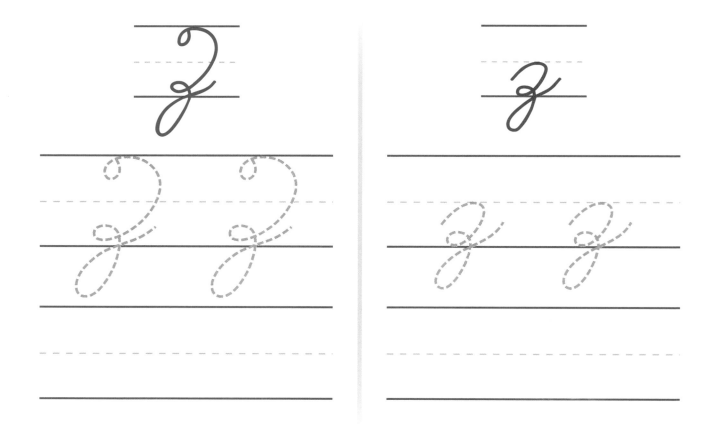

ISBN: 978-1-897457-69-6

zipper

Find and trace the hidden letters.

ISBN: 978-1-897457-69-6

ISBN: 978-1-897457-69-6

broccoli   *celery*   *eggplant*   *pumpkin*   *tomato*

Vegetables

Trace and write the words.

tomato

tomato

tomato

ISBN: 978-1-897457-69-6

broccoli

broccoli

broccoli

ISBN: 978-1-897457-69-6

broccoli | celery | eggplant | pumpkin | tomato

celery

celery

celery

ISBN: 978-1-897457-69-6

eggplant

eggplant

| *broccoli* | *celery* | *eggplant* | *pumpkin* | *tomato* |

pumpkin

pumpkin

pumpkin

ISBN: 978-1-897457-69-6